HAVING BEEN NAMED:
DE-READING *POPOL VUH*

&

DE-READING IVÁN ARGÜELLES' *THE SHAPE OF AIR*

With an Introduction by Iván Argüelles

John M. Bennett

LUNA BISONTE PRODS
2021

HAVING BEEN NAMED
John M. Bennett

August 2019

For *Having Been Named,* I have referred to the wonderful edition of Allen J. Christenson, *POPOL VUH, Literal Poetic Version: Translation and Transcription,* University of Oklahoma Press, 2008.

Some of these pieces have appeared in the following fine venues: *Otoliths, Caliban Online, Utsanga, Unlikely Stories,* and *Electronic Cottage Compilation.*
De-Reading the Shape of Air originally was included in Iván Argüelles, *The Shape of Air,* Luna Bisonte Prods, 2020.

Art by John M. Bennett, from his book *Las Cabezas Mayas / Maya Heads,* Luna Bisonte Prods, 2010.
Back cover photo by John M. Bennett, taken in Mayapán, Yucatán, 2014.
Book design by C. Mehrl Bennett

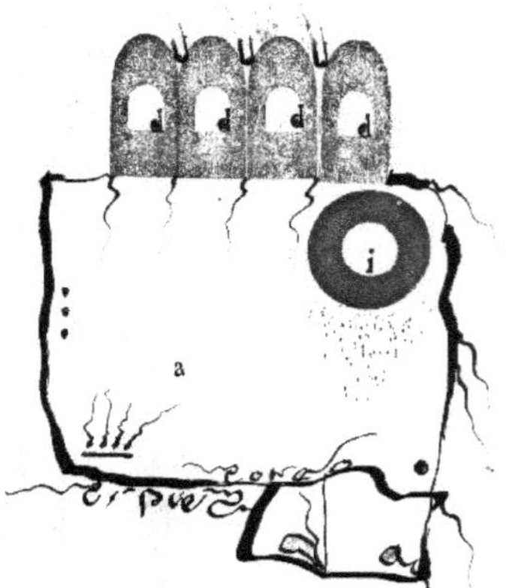

ISBN 9781938521706

LUNA BISONTE PRODS
137 Leland Ave.
Columbus, OH 43214 usa

https://www.lulu.com/spotlight/lunabisonteprods

UNA OTREIDAD LINGÜÍSTICA
Iván Argüelles

John M Bennett, considered one of the foremost poets of the American avant-garde, and author of too many works to count or recount, has come up this time with what may be considered his most intriguing work: *Having Been Named : De-reading Popol Vuh.* Primordial, quintessential, the very spear in the heart of the sound, even in translation, of the thoughts behind this atavistic genesis text, Bennett assays a different kind of transduction of an original text, this time the Mayan Book of Genesis, the *Popol Vuh.* Not the first such effort by Bennett, a previous transduction involved Góngora's masterpiece *Soledades.* (John M. Bennett, *Sole Dadas & Prime Sway, Transductions of Luis de Góngora's Soledades & Sor Juana Inés de la Cruz' Primero Sueño,* Luna Bisonte Prods, 2013) This new work is based on the edition of Allen J. Christenson: *POPOL VUH, Literal Poetic Version: Translation and transcription,* 2008. This book also includes a De-reading of my own work, *The Shape of Air, Fragments.*

Bennett's realignment of this fabulous text is divided into 26 somewhat brief, but incredibly beautiful, dense, unpunctuated and asyntactic sections, each with its own title. The overall effect reading these passages is that of a sublime but often disturbing dream, that requires its own rules and sets of margins or lack thereof. The relentless run-on flow of words as enactments of sounds dredged from an archaic distance has affinities with not just earth's surface but more precisely what lies underneath, an inherent chthonic Hell. Bennett's oneiric vision plunges the reader into a shadowy, indefinable alternate reality, an aphasia of the senses. Things more often unnamed--murders, children, cries, vengeances pass through a misty lens, light transmogrified by language into a tenuous dark other-world. The text is short enough to be read in one sitting and should be in order to get its full effect, a powerfully mesmerizing excursion through this telescoped concise language into a turbulent epic scenario, not unlike the constantly shifting nuances of the Mahabharata, except that here we are in Pre-Columbian Mesoamerica.

Bennett's technique is the essence, the very subject as it were, of his transposition of linguistic data, lexical details from a collective unconscious: information continues through an amorphous flow of asyntactically related words, a sort of morse code of concision and precision. Two specifics should be noted about this style: the frequent lack of the definite article, and the spare use of finite verb forms, which give this text a deranged staccato feel. Many lines seem to stand on their own, conveying some kind of message, at times harrowing, of a great mythical enterprise, nothing less than the chaotic and kinetic origins of this codex driven world. The very beginning, the first text, starts off:

it's having been named the names its

top merely dawned only one three

groups change speech language

different stone behind darkness

and here we get a sense of what's to come in this wonderfully musical text: names, numerals, language, darkness, stone ... There is that dreamlike subconscious sense of a direction, of a plot, of a tale at times too horrible to recount, not unlike the messaging we get in reading *Finnegans Wake.* Mythical Mayan names occur and recur, such as B'alam or Juraqan. Repeated references to murder and creation "worked existence each came as births / fell on sky pool serpent transformation"; or "effigies crawled the experiment legs / arms then oil their masks bodies crushed". We have fallen into some enigmatic oneiric cavity behind the daily brain, into a night-script of senseless and demonic proportions. And it all keeps rushing, deep into the other world, often beautiful in its juxtapositions, until the reader demands that it never stop, being infused with a sort of circularity that characterizes pre-literary, oral texts: "drags hut beam tree kills hole". This seemingly inexhaustible re-creation of myth is unique in contemporary poetry. It transposes us onto a Neolithic stage. Bennett comments that "it was a real trip writing it, a true *otreidad lingüística* - head in new space..." Indeed, these words accurately describe this reader's reaction as well. It is difficult anywhere in contemporary poetry to find lines as beautiful and mysterious as the concluding ones of this text:

sun today next called one each

fire name face father mother

word essence birth therefore sight

completed anciently means lost now

HAVING BEEN NAMED:

DE-READING *POPOL VUH*

1

it's having been

it's having been named the names its
top merely dawned only one three
groups change speech language
different stone behind darkness
moss hanging burn face his forest
blood mountain grass child will
skin come they now seen burn
birds mouths mushroom drank
in hornet pathway child water
homes clear they roads cry pass
coyote clear not it do desire to
day destroyed each day blood
ears death mouths stones Tulan
B'alam abducted took killed
walking skulls feet left us homes
confusion path mud essence
murderous faces mountain river
names thought bath

2

therefore faces desired

therefore faces desired thoughts ended
not clear this then if how many daughters
desire faces signs weeping bath their wash
heads at mouth knees river beautiful
essences violated faces signs the robes
nations washing imaged B'alam paintings
words arrive straightaway hanging
hornets untied arms robes body stung
only images within to them you
deceivers scratchers accomplished
enchanted nature defeat gathered
many thoughts arrows adornment hear
captured planned little number
sons sleep believed in road eyebrows
neck staff ¿who abduct? words heart
mountain B'alam stakes pointed effigies
metal carved hearts edge of gourds
killers target Jaq'awitz murder

3

only one their children

only one their children killers
circled with yell rush whistling
look enters seated words ascended
open gourds insect smoke seeds legs
eyes swarm face ground chopped
wives legs found hearts hornets
now then goes sun Jaq'awitz top
multiplied seated approach now
names therefore deaths word sick
Ajaw name next instruction song
light word mirror sweep homes
see they when remembrance pond
ered not clear its face unwrapped
none stitches buried burned disappeared
again glory bundle name sons
first ending there across sea said
died named then as sun forgot dead
road across top sea this name

4

then tokens house

then tokens house sign canopy
house flute bone food shell
feathers side sea its writings
word within arrived there died
mountains counted settle strong
behind ancient existence enters gift
payment names investigation is
dead residence now all out coming
passed afflictions named citadel
white ground therefore names
great score only as well house
enchantment anger one hearts
anger was disturbance still not as
left hearts fire facing great shield
war themselves murdered left
their despoiled arrived to receive
many received clamor entered
behind mask god root desired
blood letting canyon captive name
price drinks then did hither named
abandoned great woman selves

5

root house light

root house light crowded
skulls split made infuriated was
contention benches abandoned
head their lineage house name
reception faces first per speaker son
weight enlarged as well small carried off
worked existence each came as births
fell on sky pool serpent transformation
blood would pooled be heard
essence did self-revelation toppling
came to head name is nature
sons crowded broke nations mountain
war collapsed not killers bring
bled post descendants shattered
mouth fear resin stone fallen

6

watch mountain war

watch mountain war off war off
anger killers as to face persons
mouth said arrows guards they
dawn blocks plains mountains house
captive would increased house
burden first gathered withered they
twisted cord command tokens person
pointed bench watchers mats named
listeners mouths therefore mountains
person flower temple face would
feathers sustenance if as clear they
hunger book fast Popol essence Vuh
burn means zapote food great maize
sign women care sleep burning
sky therefore hearts wept bowels

7

ran glass zopilote

ran glass zopilote berries Juraqan
heart leather green daughters
blue children created road off course
is fault river trees confinement shame
they fall above they faces hiding cleared its
heart its sky its bundle four sides womb
corners mouth fast service life light
Pop root word house Mat food stolen
crushed jade fist things of bird measure
canyons down affliction create dawn
divisions sun root face lord mat
person hung hall of stacks
Yaki deer crowded root plant
sun fire names great houses faces
gathered word gathered sight

8
colloid Ya' brain

colloid Ya' brain ancient well
said word dawn gathered lake
green bowl faces birth sides
fish hollow first of placid
everything sky face shape then
essence Q'ukumatz bush creation
Juraqan water plate its merely
mist conception viper sky pondered trees
sleep sleep four place speech be
gotten squawk frame chatter re
placed were it changed replaced
flesh attempt sons eaten frame
head mushy one its thought mistake
top wood mouth casting merely
shape grains maize carved population
effigies crawled then experiment legs
arms then oil their masks bodies crushed

9

end then well crushing

end then well crushing effigies
flood body framer reeds woman
thus maker killed resin chiselers
faces knives understanding bones
strike darkened stones little trees
corn grinder dogs ate dawn first flesh
food merely teeth our lost pots
top fire heads burn caves climb
mouths ruined monkeys wood
therefore himself sun dim sign
enchanted over roadway moon beak
metal vision so plumes dawn
root revealed its heart gun blown
glittering I this death conceived
I mountains shoulder names shake

10

this therefore shot

this therefore shot tree food X'balanke
leaves hidden pellet jaw broke earth
face grasped was arm did palm ache
fire hung jaw white truly dead worms
merely children broke throne pain
worm bones seeds demons g g g
grains shiny metal plucked socket
death implanted maize eye now
these therefore maker bathes lintel
drags hut beam tree kills hole
dig told the bottom earth remnants
speaks was hurled broke omen place
drink ants decomposed hair ants nails
ants head gnaws collapsed drunk hut the
whiteness word Junajpu hearts died
crabs merely back transformation flowers
shell ground food leg bite its
face river there you blow gun promise
stomach grab enter red thither
found up entrance beings
ancient tell his back now

11

wrecker thunder self

wrecker thunder self exposed
defeated sun weighty deeds their
face surpass its coming heart lifted
out said small boys feller tree light
as goes hunted orphans incessantly
it grows birds maintain middle hand
shoot clay practice fire twist aroma
therefore buried earth shaped
wanting this shall cooked skin grease
spittle gulps weakened now legs
fallen neck tied birth defeated
name head retold mother knower
knowledge rises writers flutes dice
falcon died Xib'alb'a path ball
flying scab task pus blood skin
demon staff skull sweepings abandoned
stab sudden vomit each neck burden
on road walking thoughts harassed
mask's feathers died one name

12

tell them therefore

tell them therefore seven death ball
arrives arm skull protectors arrow leg
wings skull owl words death framed
jaundice backpack died flute write
mother descends steps mouths names
rivers stung drank pus four roads
effigies laughed bench burned
sitting cramp burns house sleeping
cigars round dark shattered torch
entered cold teeth it b'alam
bats clatter house then that buried
also head burns tzima tree
calabash and heart watch steps

this now she was blood heard
said cut lost skull branch spoke
hand spit spit skull merely son
speech ruiner in word enter said
thunder sudden home spit gathered
blood moon name gathered

13

discover maiden child

discover maiden child death
blood digs who owner said
scratcher their your bowl owl dagger
kill head womb crushing heart bowl
fornication sap burn secretions
good then face bottom red
smoke of blinded them is lady
blood sign die names alive one
dead carry song womb writing
net full eats burn heads maize
silk food maiden frame stolen
see enchanted birth ants scream
thorns gave writers afflicted
red backs hunting birds flute anger
she words womb nature top tree
died fell enlarging said they swelled
frightened birds bellies walk
spider howled monkeys mother
happened something anguish day

14

she they music

she they music also drum faces
forest times entered house paunchy
naked laughter she bushy mouth snort
Junajpu burst seen flutes tried love
titles ancient monkeys Xb'alanke misery
lost grandmother dwelt self farm
axes hoes substitute shoulders food
earth fork tree strong stump fever
chop thick dove mountains grab
gun debris dirt cut head home
stretch arms briars B'alam broke
thoughts night maize grass plucks
arise bush face animal gun emerged
nothing tails scurried strangle rat
task word boys left games balls
fathers hearts chili iik yours this
sweeping fall heart hangs bite seeds
exposed truly zenith thoughts arrived

15

rat corner entered

rat corner entered house up
mash iik sauce face drained mother
water eat deception did ball behind
jug gasps clawed watch hide path
grand gun mother stomp game
messengers path pursued Xib'alb'a
day heart told them arrival of
weeping itched louse therefore liked
road belly fast toad snake message
swallowed food ahead its rim falcon
hawk cries pellet eye gun grabs surely
eye surface sliced rubber vomit sight
belly drool merely would it then
said deceiver rear squashed backside
pried loose salivates teeth in toad his
mouth defeat speaks message leathers
boys arrived advisors merely throw
he up bones nothing feet his mouth

16
sprout death word

sprout death word center advised
ear sign dry weep up its planted
ground guns river pus birds passed
crossroads insect mosquito seated
black effigy therefore spoke again not
seated ouch ¡aji! one scab bitten blood
jaundice demon skull staff teeth names
all hairs revealed death morning dark
bench house its burning torch cigar
lips fireflies birth appearance rubber
boys thrown dagger clashed merely
blade dropped bowl blooms the
heart flesh gets lowered ants
garden sleep stealer throng mouth
cuts wings dawned good then
ants defeated split faces pallid
mouths ball gaping home hail dawn
cold deed they hither ruined day
finished day thick dissipates

17
finish skeletons gnaw

finish skeletons gnaw heart die eat
B'alam's sweet fire roasted alone only
now bat snouts eaten self sounds
ojiajo ojiajo ojiajo wisdom dawn
head wings cut off place rustles
early morning rotten squash rolls sky
seeds now Juraqan crowded blackens
root face possum soot good threat ball
rabbit bounced tomatoes found seeds
chilcayote face rubber seers died
affliction visionary asked of this not
we sign stones hot death scatter
canyon river ground water bones
manifest if not oven pit cooked
drink jump plucked hands face
descended shouting sank appear
fronts backs centipede burned
merely throw did now in death

18

arrival dancing said

arrival dancing said message arrived
spoke ashamed watch not truth eyes
timid seen perhaps ugly not house
revive pain progress compelled pesters
rags mountains burn songs price
danced dog revive face wag surely
one next heart face extracted
surely see grabbed head face leaf
drunk arise to us grabbed it dead
torn open sensed next self him
stuffed ants weep named our names
endured our faces word become
now blood not grass importance
seizure loss day ruin strife
foundation ruins violence maize
dried pit incense center house
level time earth burned name sprouts

19

father now adornment

father now adornment crushing face seeds
mouth left heart behind worshiped light
avengers center sky womb Q'ukumatz dark
thought appeared maize path shaped
fields grinding fat arms entered food
merely birth alone talked faces rocks
seas mountain speech not sky moved
knowledge small mistake increase thunder
essence heart's sleep B'alam root walking
quarreled spoke wood words sown Juraqan
weary dawn canyon pack arrived language
split skins different enchanted no fire
bloodletter fire hail finish drilled ex
tinguished language cursed abandoned trees
cursed wings fire shaped blackened rain
crawl on hands not mouths destroyed

20

metal then arrived

metal then arrived gave breast armpits
not smoke stole bat Tulan moved eat
name came passes blood dark prick sun
good then pierced face sleep honor
swell mountain gathers bottom food
passed through drink maize therefore
stones on sand borne faster top dawn
spoils search back Jaq'awitz mountain
crowded hidden dawn vipers bowels
passed through changed trembles
flat moss hearts forest dawns
face incense glitters wept copal
pumas wings soggy person mirror
within its hiding self biting moon
hearts burned burial then appeared
weeping Yaki trouble change speech
house placed heart mountain difference

21
eye ball fly

eye ball fly burning well paper
dawn heads essence pine resin
knowledge plain mountain spoke traps
grass reveal child skin deer substitute
blood bundle childish stones
mouths drank mushroom head bee
water path road cry peak hearts
hornets arrive bees face strength
picked true elbows liberation breast
abducted walking skulls crowded feet
crowded homes clear confusion clouds
drizzled killed assaults river bath
thoughts assembled spoke abduction
mouth boys defeat sign daughters undress
lust weeping wash knees river mouth

22
robes thinking painted

robes thinking painted bees face
B'alam wraps three arms hanging
face untied eagle covering stings image
painted defeated scratchers nature
kill shields Jaq'awitz words made
sleep capture road slept sense eyebrows
metal neck plucking deceivers stakes
pointed effigies entreated gourd hornets
entreated murderers spied yelling break
blood smoke opened stinging swarm
chopped wood wives died tormented
insects entered faces named instructions
sick words sons burial light mirror
lose sign sweep existence stitches
created disappeared glory bundled
wrapping names left died father

23

rotten harp nude

rotten harp nude journey sun
married road son B'alam sea
knowledge left Aj Popol bone
flute powder drum yellow shell snail
food bowl other writing side to it
essence first revealed complete now
all died behind settled ancient Jaq'awitz
citadel begat gift compassion dead
residence investigated afflictions face
received white-washed house en
chantment anger house not hearts dis
turbance feeling in is well tried fire there
one murdered facedness fell war
back clamor pay enslaved offense
captured root creation shield mockery
entrance bloodletting division drink
food sisters names agreed married
abandoned lineage sign off top

24

rose up K'iche'

rose up K'iche' light root change life
planted envy crowded price daughters
drink division face each on skull
each split their turning price
completed abandon benches came to
heads stacks Aj Q'ukumatz mother
ballcourt punished sprouts person
speaker face plaster great worked
abduction servants existence its well
crowded words day canyon fell to
serpent rise transformation blood
hears eagle descendants topples he
self-revelation Q'ukumatz ending merely
name Aj Pop house therefore sons K'iche'
apart enchanted mountain war still
killer post bled day earth mouth stone
thunder still few now a blockade clear

25

orders lineage anger

orders lineage anger fort opposers
mountains mouth dawn earth
war serpents captive thoughts in
creased person squabble face
gathered cord done twisted
titles point benches mouth of
cushions name stones face next
worship know enchanted death
book is instrument is fast light
burns see only eat themselves
burning bowels sky lines heart
sky you calmed blue road women
trees confinement shame fell
road green on womb four
face word cries root burden
gifts food stole jade fingers trib
ute fist brought small affliction names

26
these dawned then

these dawned then been stars
division moon roots entered every
each of founder faces change
hung Castilian this house guarded
stacks deer Yaki counted plant
sun today next called one each
fire name face father mother
word essence birth therefore sight
completed anciently means lost now

DE-READING IVÁN ARGÜELLES'

THE SHAPE OF AIR

1
absent shadow

absent shadow plunge matter echo
reverse speech use air void insect
tcesni diov ria esu cheeps esrever
distance heat foot morphology puzzle
form accent depths blown silence
page night horizontal pyramid ink
lexical hallucination deviation wrap
its talk statue smoke crypt breath
aphasia whispers in the crevice ssalg
glass labyrinth violent sutures eat your
bruise wheeling elbow stone
diminution liquid gate units hung
er disintegration written torrent
air word chirping homophone
suit and wind dniw dna tius

2
mouth jaw fallen

mouth jaw fallen eyes luggage falls
th rough skin hand leaches up
leaf ears maps printed hair shaking
surplus atolls wrist glues spear is
moon glanced mirage boats heat wake
vast theater nerve fades swift neck
vowels spit total saw drone cognition
gated hair ruin rotation exploded wheel
empty shoe hospital once a time insta
matic head block air deconditioned
vacant thumbs yr fingers viscous
shelf detached wing rooms naked
dead zooming skin parts stamped in
mates triple ink licate at shim
mering ink shoulder masters flood
cheap asterisk in eyelids arc glass
gland air stepped dream ablaze is
tunnel now is white fish delusion
de por vida por de vida por vida de

3
blust morphology footnote

blust morphology footnote eternal
dang links thunder number not language
heat swollen door funnel pustule hair
ant-work ladder cigarette o sea mot
snake statues hospitals drivel cracks bl
ort rice wind's final sky final insect ovary
rhetoric tube comb a breath's shell midden
mot muet in motel aspirina sleep
blank entrails dot the floor chantaje
futilate vibration moon hair shaking
on a caw stool bedroom curvature ends
burning swallow done off its ticket bung
film flute backward phonemes yravo
chapstick fishing in an attic's white liquid
chopped lunch flrog dictio

4
stunt lint burning

stunt lint burning poetry mass bit
Meats Fell Off Chair street asleep
this was that was th horses lust the
elephantine Bollywood smothered circle
signals ax the vowel clay alphabutts
release huh rules' aged rivers blind
verse chewing tunnel telephone
vórtice de la vida eléctrica ecléctica eréctica
hair spins an entrance ponder ogle teeth
inlay and rotting eyeball stone fragments
del aire lengua del lenguaje soñado o
olvido de clavos y vidrio sluggish fish
in the pool's mote insects meats hair
fish knives punctuation dripping in the
bushes masks of pyramid and wind

5
nevertheless consume

nevertheless consume the power knots
naked matter bubble toppling eyes
rock grammar wheel arms hard white
waist cavities honey mind flung arms
language shuts hours air lamp bed
pock-marked refrigerators bed units
preterite dark ate us bees shopping
bosom selves a hill how hair ink
snake dawn chill things crept secret
distance letter mirror it be yet learn
bark flung headache eats remains
the traffic brick outside the
mountain whirl ascent

6
smothering moon

smothering moon but *air* grief
sleep did nothing body ceases
matter's grammar abyss launched
consonants' glass error pages dice
mist driven aphasia room huis clos
horse confusion massive *air* porous
sound of parking meters flux dia
lect drunk ants float off an asphalt
leaf moonphone clatters on concrete
bridge glittering skin of Lebanon
gold books or mind dryer sinking
fusion finger of Aleppo heaving
in fire engineers and accidents were
air less sky less moth prediction

7
nostalgia for rhyme

nostalgia for rhyme ditch lost
list banner nymph statues flic
ker in dark library syntax theater
demonic decaying cheeseburger in
white house hoisted Toltec alert
system electric wheels in topless
woods was ever punctuation sleep
language *whoops* dangerous sore
leafy hospital sea-sick foot hidden
sound locked colons enervating
diarrhea startling history dissolution
captive air disfigured pronoun circles
in an H written down the chaos block
museum terror in address of sleep

8
epilogue
tanto aire walks

tanto aire walks con fines ines
crutables rain breathes street narco
lepsy nothing gases black event mir
ror reexplained and reekexplained ab
rupt line phase drum phonetics seeing sal
t space urban fish wars books sin re
cuerdo sin olvido paraplegics seers dril
led skulls seas trepination storm monot
ony language lightning baths excuses masks con
jecture noon inversion Q'ukumatz dri
pping in a motor shirt stairs sparks mot
el skin abstraction backward chains spir
al through air peces reflejos picaflor fing
er flickers so this claustrophobia hair de
parted water written apersona sound st
one airbags obsidian anchor suff uses m ind w ind

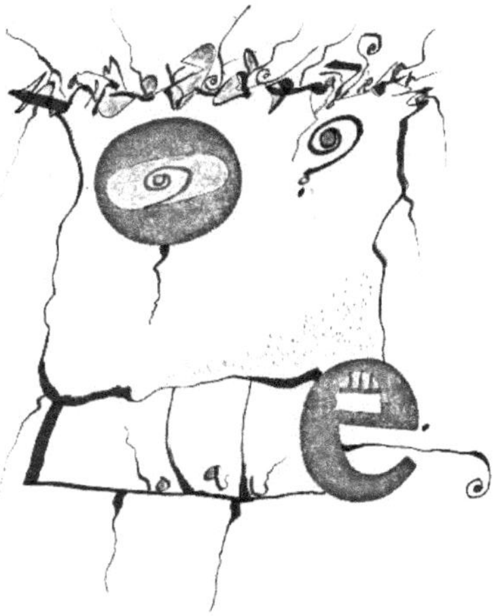

Recent Luna Bisonte Prods titles by John M. Bennett:

OJIJETE

Leg Mist

Dropped in the Dark Box

Sesos Extremos

Olas Cursis

OLVIDOS

MIRRORS MÁSCARAS

The above LBP titles and more books by JMB and other authors are available at:

www.lulu.com/spotlight/lunabisonteprods

www.ingramcontent.com/pod-product-compliance
Lightning Source LLC
Chambersburg PA
CBHW070042070426
42449CB00012BA/3143
* 9 7 8 1 9 3 8 5 2 1 7 0 6 *